12/16

OLIVER SACKS

OLIVER SACKS
THE LAST INTERVIEW
and OTHER CONVERSATIONS

MELVILLE HOUSE
BROOKLYN • LONDON

OLIVER SACKS: THE LAST INTERVIEW AND OTHER CONVERSATIONS

First Melville House printing: November 2016

"Neurologist Oliver Sacks" was originally broadcast on *Fresh Air* on October 1, 1987. Reprinted with permission by WHYY/NPR.

"An Anthropologist on Mars" was originally broadcast on *Charlie Rose* in February 1995. Reprinted with permission by *Charlie Rose*/PBS.

"Studs, Sacks, and Left-Handed Skills" was originally broadcast on *The Studs Terkel Program* in 1995. Courtesy of the Studs Terkel Radio Archive.

"Oliver Sacks on Empathy as a Path to Insight" was published in the November 2010 issue of *Harvard Business Review*. Reprinted with permission.

"The Joy of Aging" was originally broadcast on *On Point* on July 18, 2013. Reprinted with permission by WBUR/NPR.

"Dr. Sacks Looks Back" was recorded live with Robert Krulwich at the Brooklyn Academy of Music on May 5, 2015. Reprinted with permission by *Radiolab*/WNYC studios.

Some of these interviews were transcribed and have been lightly edited for clarity.

Melville House Publishing		8 Blackstock Mews
46 John Street	and	Islington
Brooklyn, NY 11201		London N4 2BT

mhpbooks.com   facebook.com/mhpbooks   @melvillehouse

Library of Congress Cataloging-in-Publication Data
Names: Sacks, Oliver, 1933-2015, author. | Sacks, Oliver, 1933-2015,
    interviewee.
Title: Oliver Sacks : the last interview and other conversations.
Description: Brooklyn : Melville House, 2016.
Identifiers: LCCN 2016041051 (print) | LCCN 2016041462 (ebook) | ISBN
    9781612195773 (paperback) | ISBN 9781612195780 (ebook)
Subjects: LCSH: Sacks, Oliver, 1933-2015,–Interviews. | Neurologists–
    England–Interviews. | Neurologists–United States–Interviews. | BISAC:
    BIOGRAPHY & AUTOBIOGRAPHY / Literary. | BIOGRAPHY &
    AUTOBIOGRAPHY / Medical.
Classification: LCC RC339.52.S23 A36 2016 (print) | LCC RC339.52.S23
    (ebook) | DDC 616.80092 [B] –dc23
LC record available at https://lccn.loc.gov/2016041051

Printed in the United States of America

1   3   5   7   9   10   8   6   4   2

CONTENTS

EDITOR'S NOTE

Dr. Oliver Sacks was "morbidly shy," as one of the interlocutors in this collection notes—which may be why there were relatively few formal interviews with the great neuroscientist, physician, and bestselling author.

It's rather surprising, considering Sacks's long career and prolific output. Between 1970 and 2015, he wrote fourteen books, including *Awakenings* (which was adapted into a film starring Robin Williams), the blockbuster *The Man Who Mistook His Wife for a Hat*, and *On the Move*, a memoir published just six months before his death in August 2015. He was also a regular contributor to *The New Yorker*, *The New York Review of Books*, and the *London Review of Books*, among other publications.

For the most part, what seems to have convinced Sacks to grant interviews was the obligation to promote his work, and so the rarities collected herein were each conducted to coincide with the publication of a book and were broadcast on major programs such as Charlie Rose's PBS television show, National Public Radio's *Fresh Air* program, and the beloved icon Studs Terkel's radio show. They are primarily accessible in audio format, and several were transcribed here for the first time by Melville House.

In these transcriptions, we endeavored to preserve Sacks's verbal characteristics—for example, his charming tendency to stutter and to often qualify his comments with the disclaimer "sort of." Readers will also notice that some interviewers interrupt more than others (indicated with an em dash), and some are decidedly unhurried, relishing contemplative pauses (indicated with an ellipsis).

The first interview, the first of several Sacks had with *Fresh Air*'s Terry Gross, offers an introduction to the doctor's uniquely literary approach to his work—"describing states of mind as well as neurological conditions." Both of the interviews that follow—with Charlie Rose and Studs Terkel, respectively—were released after the publication of the book *An Anthropologist on Mars*, but they take distinct approaches to their subject. The Rose interview is more obviously personal, even philosophical: Sacks discusses his family, his friendship with Robin Williams, his appreciation of the brain as an "unimaginably complex and beautiful" part of who we are, and his longing for faith in a

God he cannot, in the end, believe exists. The interview with Terkel, meanwhile, hews closely to the book itself, but in doing so reveals the inner workings of the author, whom Terkel introduces as "a wonder of a neurologist, who has the soul of a poet but the writing gifts of a fine novelist."

The remaining interviews—with Lisa Burrell for the *Harvard Business Review*, Tom Ashbrook for NPR's *On Point*, and Robert Krulwich for NPR's *Radiolab*—were all conducted after Sacks was diagnosed with ocular cancer in 2005. They address mortality more directly, and explore the ways in which Sacks's relationships to his patients had changed, now that he was a patient as well. Ashbrook's interview was conducted shortly after Sacks's eightieth birthday, when he'd been inspired to write an op-ed for *The New York Times* about his contentedness in old age ("I can write up a storm, and I can swim up a storm . . . I think swimming is one of the few activities one can do for the first century").

The final interview was presented to a live audience at the Brooklyn Academy of Music on May 5, 2015, after *Radiolab*'s host Robert Krulwich had visited Sacks and recorded their conversation in his home. It is by far the most poignant in the collection. Sacks was keenly aware that this interview was to be among his last. Of his latest diagnosis, Sacks said, "One or two people have written to me, you know, consoling me, and said, 'Well, you know, we all die.' But fuck it! It's not like, *We all die*. It's like, *You have four months*." It's poignant, too, for the decades-long friendship between Krulwich and

Sacks, which is evoked in the candor and wonderful intimacy of their dialogue.

The conversations collected herein, then, span nearly thirty years and cover a range of topics, but they are unified by the spirit of warmth, empathy, and ingenious curiosity for which Sacks was so famous and rightly beloved.

OLIVER SACKS

NEUROLOGIST OLIVER SACKS

INTERVIEW WITH TERRY GROSS
FRESH AIR
OCTOBER 1, 1987

GROSS: Dr. Oliver Sacks, welcome to *Fresh Air*.

SACKS: Nice to be here.

GROSS: Before we talk about the medical and spiritual implications of the work that you do, I'm going to ask you to tell the story of "The Man Who Mistook His Wife for a Hat," one of the case studies that you've written about. This was a music teacher and singer who didn't recognize that he *had* a disorder. What were the symptoms that he was showing?

SACKS: Um, well, the first problem was that he had difficulty recognizing his students at the music academy. As soon as they spoke, he recognized them at once, but he couldn't recognize them visually. And soon he couldn't' recognize anyone or anything visually. He couldn't recognize his wife, he couldn't recognize himself, he couldn't recognize common objects. He saw them perfectly clearly, but what he saw carried no meaning for him. And no sense. And this prompted him to sort of ingenious but sometimes wild and sometimes absurd guesses as to what he might be seeing.

GROSS: And you title the case study "The Man Who Mistook His Wife for a Hat" because in reaching for his hat, he reached for his wife's head by mistake.

SACKS: Well, when I saw him in the first interview, he was obviously not demented, but a delightful, intelligent, civilized man with a sense of humor. He kept encountering the fact that he made mistakes, but he didn't recognize what the problem was. It mixed with all his intact-ness. There was a succession of absurd mistakes. At one point, he confused his left foot with his shoe and he didn't seem to know which was which, and then right at the end when he went to reach for his hat, he got his wife's head instead.

GROSS: What is the condition that he had?

SACKS: Well, this is called a visual agnosia. And what happens is that the normal meeting between visual input, between images and the person's memories and, um, ideas, feelings, and expectations doesn't occur. And so this goes with a problem in the visual association areas at the back of the brain. So he sort of had raw vision, a sort of raw seeing which didn't ascend into the realm of meaning.

GROSS: Although he couldn't make sense of what he saw, he was a musician and singer and he still had perfect musical sense, and your prescription to him was music. Why?

SACKS: Well, he was really absolutely lost in this meaning-less, shattered visual world, and he desperately needed some way of organizing himself. Now, I think all of us tend to either use internal speech or internal music to organize ourselves to some extent. One has things like nursery rhymes—"One, two, buckle my shoe"—or marching songs, or work songs, but the *song* as a unit of organization became tremendously important and crucial for this man who was so totally lost visually, couldn't use any visual organization but in fact was a marvelous musician and singer, a man who sort of generated songs all the while. And one saw again and again that he couldn't do it, he couldn't shave, he couldn't eat, unless he really set the activity to music internally. On one occasion when he was eating there were interruptions: the postman suddenly knocked at the door, and this completely shattered the activity. He was quite bewildered for a few seconds before he was able to recapture the melody of eating.

GROSS: You know your prescription of music reminds me of something your friend the poet W. H. Auden had said to you, which is that, um, well he spoke of the poetic and the religious states of affliction, and I wonder what you think, how that applies to your work. The poetic and religious states of affliction.

SACKS: I thought you were going to actually quote one of Auden's favorite quotations from Novalis, where Novalis says, "Every disease has a musical problem, and every cure has a musical solution." And certainly with Dr. P, as with many of my Parkinsonian patients—people sometimes who can't move unless they sing or dance—one sees absolutely they've been "un-music-ed" by disease and can be "re-music-ed" back into health.

I think that the poetic and the religious are almost sometimes an integral part of patients' perceptions, as to what may be happening with them. Something I describe in the *Hat* book, and also at more length in an earlier book, *A Leg to Stand On*, is a patient whom I saw as a student, who had apparently lost his left leg. He was found on the floor, very bewildered; he had apparently thrown himself out of bed in a peculiar way, and the story he gave was that he had woken up from sleep. He had found that there was a foreign leg in the bed with him, disgusting object. He threw it out, then, now horribly, he had come out with it, and now it was attached to him. And I said, "But it's your leg." And he said, "Shouldn't I know my own leg?" And I said, "Yes, you should." And he said, "Well, I know it's *not* my leg." Now this thing for him was not only . . . was terribly wrong. It felt ugly, it felt hateful, it felt obscene, it felt unholy, it felt an offense against nature.

Now, the particular physiology in his case was that he had a tumor in the opposite side of the brain which had expanded, which had bled while he slept, and had blotted out the part of the brain which represents the leg, so the leg image had been obliterated. Therefore, he could not recognize his leg as his own. Therefore, it seemed absolutely other. But the "absolutely other" always seems uncanny, and horrible, and obscene, and unholy, and godforsaken . . . and words like this, or concepts like this, would be used by *every* patient, irrespective of background, of intelligence, of education. The alienation is almost intrinsically in the area of subjectivity, is sort of felt as anti-poetic, anti-religious. And by the same token, when it comes back, there is the feeling, to quote Dante, of the "holy and glorious flesh" restored. And so I think even at this level, sort of, the body and health is always felt as sort of beautiful and holy, although one may not appreciate this unless it's taken away, and one suddenly deals with a sort of radically depreciated world.

GROSS: Your way of writing case studies is really very literary. It's not empirical, it's not cut-and-dried. You're really describing states of mind as well as neurological conditions. And I've wondered if patients talk to you that way, if they are as descriptive as you are in telling their stories.

SACKS: I think, obviously this will depend on the condition and the patient, but above all I think of the situation, and that if a patient is not permitted, implicitly or explicitly, to talk about himself, if he's reduced, if he's given a sort of catechism—*Do you have this? Do you have that?*—then he will reduce himself to a list of symptoms. He won't say what it's actually like. He won't depict the world he is in, which he has been thrust into. But I think that if patients have a complaint, sometimes more serious or as serious as their primary complaint, it is that they can't communicate what it's like. And I think that a major act of the doctor is somehow to—Dr. Quincy once talked about "the pressure of the incommunicable upon the heart"—is to let the patient *try* to communicate, and the doctor must sort of help him, must reach out, delicately, to assist this trembling communication. And, um, so that between them, the way it is, the world of illness can come into being.

GROSS: You've done a lot of your work on back wards of hospitals, charity hospitals, asylums. Why have you gone there looking for the kinds of cases you were interested in studying?

SACKS: Well, I'm, it's really not quite in that order. I *was* there, in places which most of my colleagues wouldn't be seen *dead* in, and which no ambitious young doctor would go to, and which are felt to be the sticks. But in fact here, there is, you know, there is the priceless gift of leisure. There's no pressure to diagnose, there's no pressure to do anything. Also you can encounter a complete world. I mean these places are really little worlds. And I think an un-pressed exploration of getting deeper and deeper is possible in such places, and hardly possible in any other places.

GROSS: There's no pressure because they're considered hopeless anyways?

SACKS: Partly. This was well-realized by the founders of neurology, by Hughlings Jackson and Charcot in the last century—they spent much of their lives in chronic hospitals, institutions, asylums. But now, um, now doctors don't . . . but certainly, with the patients I describe in *Awakenings*, these people which had been in hospital for forty years or more, since the great Sleeping Sickness epidemic, I had no idea that such patients existed, that such *lives* existed, until I went into a chronic hospital.

GROSS: Has that happened other times too, that you've found disorders that have not really been described before?

SACKS: Ah, well, certainly they haven't been described with the richness and the fullness which they should have. Um, the, in general, I think description has become sort of obsolete.

GROSS: You've described it as almost a nineteenth-century art in medicine.

SACKS: I mean, I love nineteenth-century medicine and science. It may have been so short, in a way, on certain empirical remedies, and even relatively short on physiological concepts, and of course so short on technology, but the respect for the patient and for the detail of what was happening to them, I think could often generate almost, you know, novelistically rich and at the same time medically and scientifically accurate descriptions, so much so now that major discoveries have been made by going back over nineteenth-century descriptions. Now we can see what went on. I think most of the descriptions now are so meager, so threadbare, and also . . . too quick to diagnose, to pin labels on.

GROSS: When you are working with patients who have been almost abandoned by the medical profession, it's just a kind of a caretaking type of thing, are you able to do anything to really change their condition, or are you more interested in observing them? And let's leave out the Sleeping Sickness patients, because you were able to administer a drug there that totally changed their condition, but in other cases when there isn't a drug that's going to change their state, what can you do?

SACKS: Um, my first notion is to try to understand, to try to understand *with* the patient, what's going on. Now, *from* the understanding, treatment may come. So that for example with one case I describe in the *Hat* book, as I call it for short, there's a Parkinsonian man who leaned grossly to one side, although he wasn't aware of this. He was surprised that people commented. I took a videotape of this, I played it back to him, and it as only when he saw this that he realized what was happening, and he then he asked a very acute question. He said he wondered whether there were balancing mechanisms—he used to be a carpenter—like spirit levels, like bubble levels in the head which had been impaired by his disease. And I said, "Yeah, exactly." And he then thought again, and he wondered if one couldn't make such little levels outside the head, for example attached to, by a nose-clip, the glasses, and whether this would serve to balance him. And I said, that's a wonderful idea, let's try it. And in fact it worked beautifully. Now here is a man who, all I did in a sense, was to—

GROSS: Give him a metaphor!

SACKS: Um, yes, or, he gave himself a metaphor. I assisted *his* understanding, and indeed his movement to a cure. And I love this sort of collaboration, when it's possible.

GROSS: I thank you very much for talking with us about your work, thank you for being here.

SACKS: Thank you.

AN ANTHROPOLOGIST ON MARS

INTERVIEW WITH CHARLIE ROSE
CHARLIE ROSE
FEBRUARY 1995

ROSE: Oliver Sacks is here. His new book is *An Anthropologist on Mars*. He is professor of clinical neurology at Albert Einstein College of Medicine, author of *Migraine*, *Awakenings*, *The Man Who Mistook His Wife for a Hat*, and *Seeing Voices: A Journey into the World of the Deaf*, and it's a pleasure to have him back on this broadcast. Welcome.

SACKS: Thank you.

ROSE: Tell me what it is that you think that you do, because you say, in an interesting way, that what your work is about is an intersection of biology and biography. Meaning what?

SACKS: Well, I want to describe lives which have been influenced by some overwhelming neurological problem or deficit, like colorblindness or autism, but to expand it into a full biography, which involves my spending time with a person and seeing them in real life, in their homes.

ROSE: You came from a family of doctors, yes?

SACKS: Yes.

ROSE: Your brothers are doctors?

SACKS: Yes.

ROSE: Your mother and father were involved in medicine, yes?

SACKS: Right, mm-hm.

ROSE: When did you develop the interest that you have in neurology and the neurosciences?

SACKS: Well, I think in a way it was very, very early, and both my parents trained in neurology although they didn't practice it.

ROSE: Yeah.

SACKS: But the . . . the brain is the most incredible thing in the universe, and I think I probably knew from twelve or fourteen that was it.

ROSE: Was there a moment? Was there an event? Was there a thing that . . . I mean, was there a time that it happened for you? No epiphany?

SACKS: Well, there have been a lot of epiphanies, but, no, it emerged. Right.

ROSE: Yeah. Talk about some of the people here, of these

people. I mean, I . . . the characters from Temple Grandin to
Dr. Carl Bennett and Virgil and, and the others that you pro-
file here. Who is closest to you? Who is the one whose story
you find the most fascinating?

SACKS: I think probably the . . . well, I find them all fascinating.

ROSE: I know you do.

SACKS: But I think probably the first case, the case of the
colorblind painter—

ROSE: Yeah.

SACKS: —this fine artist who wrote me out of the blue, although he could no longer see blue at that time—

ROSE: Yeah.

SACKS: —saying that he'd had a head injury, and he'd suddenly lost all of his color perception. And for him, as a color
artist, this absolutely drained the meaning and feeling out of
the world, and he was sort of desperate. I'd never really thought
about color and what this might mean. And first of all, I de-
termined what, you know, what exactly had gone wrong, that
really the color parts of the brain had been knocked out.

ROSE: Yeah.

SACKS: But what seemed to me so fascinating was that

this horrible, impoverished gray world he was in gradually changed for him and became beautiful and full of meaning again, and he started painting again and sort of re-centered himself as an artist in black and white, and at that point, when we wondered whether he might want color, he said, "No. My world's complete without it." But I knew him very well, and we really became companions and friends, and he seems to me the most beautiful example of an adaptation, really, of having lost one's health and one's normality—color vision—he, he got another health.

ROSE: If you look at all the people in here, do they share any common denominator, in a sense—if you lose a sense, or if you lose something, what?

SACKS: Something else will develop and will heighten, and I think this sort of adaptational compensation probably runs through all, all seven.

ROSE: Well, take Temple Grandin for me. She gave the title to the book, yes?

SACKS: Right.

ROSE: She called herself, she felt . . . well, you describe it for me. Because I thought you might say she was the most interesting to you.

SACKS: Well, I . . . I—

ROSE: I'm not asking you to choose among your children, but—

SACKS: —no, no. I was never intending to write about her. I met her, and I was sort of swept off my feet during the weekend, and I largely wrote the piece on the journey back from Colorado.

ROSE: Why did she sweep you off her feet? Off your feet?

SACKS: Well, here's a woman who was deeply autistic at three, and sort of rocking and mute and inaccessible, and now she is this, this extraordinary sort of world expert on cattle, and highly intelligent, and yet, in a way, completely missing in the sort of social dimension. She doesn't understand people's expressions or states of mind.

ROSE: And doesn't want any human contact, does she?

SACKS: Well, I . . . no, I think she does. She's not really withdrawn, but she does say, she says she's studying us. She's studying the species—

ROSE: Yes.

SACKS: —you know, very, very closely, and then she said she felt like an anthropologist on Mars. But really, the sense of someone who, in a way, is an outsider and forced to be an outsider, but who by an immense sort of intelligence really,

really is bridging the gap: she is so different and so human, and I had never met anyone like her.

ROSE: Tell me about Virgil.

SACKS: I had a phone call telling me of Virgil. He'd been blind more or less from birth—

ROSE: Right.

SACKS: —and he was given the gift of sight when middle-aged, when he was fifty, but it didn't work. People expected either that the operation would fail or that he would emerge fully sighted, and what happened was neither. The telephone conversation said he sees everything, but he recognizes nothing. When the bandages came off, he just saw a blur of movement and color, and then there was a voice, and he knew voices came from faces, and this blur, this chaos, must be a face, but he couldn't form a perception of a face. His brain had never learned to, to deal with things . . . and so he was really thrown into a state of profound confusion, into a visual world which made no sense, somewhat like the visual world of "The Man Who Mistook His Wife for a Hat"—

ROSE: Yes.

SACKS: —but there, those parts of the brain had been destroyed. In Virgil, they'd, they'd never developed. Now, he was a brave man, and he, he sort of adventured into this, this alien chaotic world of sight, although it was full of dangers for him, and he . . . There have been very, very few cases like this, and in every case, there's a tremendous crisis because someone has been secure in the senses they have, and you can't force a new sense on anybody. I mean, it would be like forcing you suddenly . . . giving you X-ray vision.

ROSE: That would be good. What, what, what sense that you don't have, I mean, you have all the obvious senses, what power would you most like to have that you don't have, what ability would you most like to have you don't have? What skill, what insight?

SACKS: I . . . I'd like to be a mathematician sometimes. I'm not very good at maths.

ROSE: Why a mathematician?

SACKS: Because I feel this is a different way of articulating the universe, and at least the equivalent of language. And I think probably many people would be decent mathematicians if they were decently educated, but I think, I think now, with the new maths, people, people are.

ROSE: How would you measure your skill in being able to reach people—to the patients—in contrast to your skill as, as . . . your professional skill, your medical training? I mean, it, it seems to me that's what separates you, that's what gives you the gift.

SACKS: I was going to say that I would like more, more empathy, and then some—

ROSE: Yeah.

SACKS: —somehow mathematics sort of darted in.

ROSE: Yeah. But it would seem to me you are full of empathy. Are you not? I mean, are you less empathetic than we might imagine? Is this more scientific than we assume from your presence?

SACKS: No. I think that science can't simulate empathy, which is partly what, you know, what goes on with Temple. But I . . . it's a tremendous privilege, extraordinary, when people, in a way, let one, you know, they let you into themselves.

ROSE: You feel privileged that they will allow you to come inside of their own soul and emotion and being and, and share.

SACKS: Absolutely. And it's a very delicate business, but it's— and one mustn't be invasive or push—but it is like being invited into a sanctuary.

ROSE: Well, some thought you were invasive, thank you very much. In fact, it was Miriam—what was her name?—who, who didn't like the fact that you wrote about her, right?

SACKS: Oh, well, right. That was in *Awakenings*.

ROSE: Yes.

SACKS: Well, it wasn't that—

ROSE: And she found a copy of the book from England or something?

SACKS: Yes, yes.

ROSE: Wasn't it—

SACKS: Yeah, she— I tried to conceal *Awakenings* from—

ROSE: Yeah, right, right.

SACKS: —the patients, but she—

ROSE: And she didn't like the—I'm interrupting, but she— tell me why she was upset.

SACKS: Well, no. She didn't mind me telling, as it were, the tragedy of her life, but she didn't like the physical description. And—

ROSE: Can you understand that?

SACKS: I understand that very well, especially after I was profiled myself in *The New York Times*, and they said I was monstrously fat.

ROSE: Oh, my God! Did they?

SACKS: And it so annoyed—

ROSE: The big, bad *New York Times*.

SACKS: Right. It so annoyed me, I lost one hundred pounds.

ROSE: Did you keep it off?

SACKS: Yeah.

ROSE: Oh, good for you! The, the notion of the . . . *Awakenings* and, what do you think of Robin Williams? You've got to know him well. And you're going later this evening, you're going to be honored—he's being honored by some—

SACKS: Right.

ROSE: —academy here in New York. You two are friends?

SACKS: Yes, indeed.

ROSE: Yeah. Tell me about the friendship because he played you, obviously.

SACKS: Right. Well, we, we spent a lot of time together at first, and we hung out together. We went to see patients, and I thought he was just, you know, a nice, brilliant guy. I didn't realize that I was, in fact, the subject of unceasing, relentless, and at the same time very, very sympathetic observation—

ROSE: Yeah, right.

SACKS: —until I was having a conversation with him, and I got into one of my odd gestures such as you see there—

ROSE: Yeah, like this. Yes.

SACKS: Yes . . . that I seem, I seem to get into these things.

ROSE: And all of a sudden, he's watching.

SACKS: Yeah. Well, well, well, no. He was in the, in the same gesture, and he wasn't imitating me, but by that point, he had—

ROSE: He was becoming you.

SACKS: Well, exactly. He, he had my gestures. He had my opinions, my wishes, my regrets, my interests, my memories.

ROSE: Yeah, yeah.

SACKS: I mean, it was an extraordinary sort of identical, in-stant identical twin. At that point, we felt we had to make some distance between us.

ROSE: You felt or he felt, or both?

SACKS: I think . . . well, I certainly felt it. I think he felt it a bit as well.

ROSE: That he'd better pull back. He was becoming you, rather than—

SACKS: Yeah.

ROSE: —giving himself some room to create.

SACKS: Absolutely. But since then we've seen quite a lot of each other, and we, we enjoy our differentness, as well as the sort of strange convergence which once happened.

ROSE: And your differentness is simply what you do or, or something more—

SACKS: The . . . perhaps there's also something similar. I think, I think we're both sort of a bit, a bit explosive, but we're sort of complementary creatures.

ROSE: You consider Martin Buber one of your favorite writers, yes?

SACKS: Right, right.

ROSE: And, and you've taken what he says and sort of paraphrased it and translated it into, "We must humanize technology before it dehumanizes us." What's the worst fear? How does that fear manifest itself, in your judgment?

SACKS: Well, in medicine, I think the person can be replaced by the CAT scan and the EEG, which reduces the person to an object, and it reduces the physician to a technician, and I think, I think this is a great ever-present danger in medicine. But it sort of infuriates me, in a way, to have to humor my computer because—

ROSE: Yes.

SACKS: —because it's, you know, it's not like talking to someone, and—

ROSE: Yeah.

SACKS: —although perhaps computers are getting a bit—

ROSE: You have to humor it in order to—

SACKS: To use it. I mean, it forces me to do things its way.

ROSE: Otherwise, it'll cut out on you.

SACKS: Right.

ROSE: You're next going to do—you're going to go to the island of, of Pingelap.

SACKS: Well, I, I went to this little island, and I—

ROSE: This is for another book, is it?

SACKS: Yes, I think so.

ROSE: Yeah.

SACKS: This is a, a little coral atoll on the Pacific, where congenital colorblindness—being born totally colorblind, which is tremendously rare, one in 50,000 in the normal population—is common.

ROSE: So most of the people there are colorblind.

SACKS: Well, well, certainly, there, there are seventy or eighty colorblind people, and there's a, so to speak, a community who have had no concept of color for two centuries—

ROSE: Yeah.

SACKS: —and whose language and whose dress and whose horticulture—and they have, they get along fine. And I think partly they think the rest of us are suffering from sort of chromatic hallucinations.

ROSE: Well, I mean, maybe this is the reason some people like black-and-white film or something. But what, what is it that fascinates you about them? I mean, why, of all the things that you could be curious about, are you curious about them?

SACKS: I'm, I'm damned if I know, but there you are.

ROSE: But, well then, my second question is all of a sudden you went there. Didn't you do something to your—what did you do?

SACKS: Well, it's possible now, using a bit of technology—

ROSE: Yeah.

SACKS: —to, to buzz that part of the brain, which—

ROSE: You can . . . how would you do it? How would you buzz that part?

SACKS: Well, it's done with a magnetic device. It's done through the skull. It is harmless.

ROSE: Is it done one time, or done every day, or what?

SACKS: No. It, it's just done one time.

ROSE: And then, so you can—then your color perception is gone until you're buzzed again.

SACKS: Yes, perhaps for ten or twenty minutes.

ROSE: Oh.

SACKS: I want to know what Jonathan I. felt and saw. I want to know what all of my patients experience. I . . . it's not sufficient for me just to hear it and look at it. I want to sort of really dive in and experience it myself if I can. I think with this, this achromotopia, this knocking out the color areas, this one can—

ROSE: Yeah. What's . . . what areas of exploration of the brain are the most fascinating to you?

SACKS: I think increasingly those to do with consciousness. I, I've looked at sort of perception and movement for years, but now I'm interested in language and consciousness and what—

ROSE: Consciousness.

SACKS: —and what makes us a person, the neural basis of being Charlie Rose or Oliver Sacks, because you—your brain is you in a way in which your heart isn't. You could have a heart transplant. You couldn't have a brain transplant.

ROSE: I might need one, though. But go ahead.

SACKS: And, and the way in which the brain embodies the self and has been doing so from the moment of birth, and I think, I think this is the exciting thing. And, and—

ROSE: Is it—do you have a sense—am I right in assuming that we, you know, that we are just beginning to understand the brain? I mean, if you look at our analysis of how the human body works and all, we—the area that's least explored is the brain, and that has the most potential for payoff?

SACKS: Oh, oh, absolutely. I mean, I think we understand the heart or the liver or the kidney very well now. There are many further things to be learned, but with the brain, we're only starting. We have really no idea. I mean, the complexity is—you know, there are, there are sort of thousands of messages going on simultaneously between different parts of the brain. It is unimaginably complex and beautiful, and I think one hundred years from now, you know, people will still be in mid-investigation.

ROSE: Why do you like to swim so much?

SACKS: Because . . . because I'm a water creature. I'm at home in the water. I lose my self-consciousness. I feel like a porpoise. When—my father was a swimming champ. He threw us all in when we were babies, and so I have always swum.

ROSE: Yeah.

SACKS: And—

ROSE: Someone said to you, "You become—you transform yourself from a difficult, hesitant, geriatric terrestrial form to a fluid, beautiful porpoise form."

SACKS: Right. And I also . . . I do a lot of my thinking in the water. Once I can get into a sort of trance-like state, and then the, the thoughts flow like the water, and I'd, I'd like to be in the water—

ROSE: Yeah.

SACKS: —all day.

ROSE: You don't believe in—I mean, you're not strongly religious. You don't believe in God.

SACKS: I can't imagine what, what is meant. No, I, I guess I don't. I would like to. I mean, I pine for a creator and a protector. I look at sort of Giotto's paintings, and I think what we've missed. But I can't—I think the universe has organized itself and is organizing itself without, without any help or any surveillance.

ROSE: Evolution speaks to you.

SACKS: Yeah. And yet, it—that can't be satisfying in, you know, in the human way of a God, and I think this is, this is just what one has to put up with.

ROSE: Oliver Sacks. *An Anthropologist on Mars.*

STUDS, SACKS, AND LEFT-HANDED SKILLS

INTERVIEW WITH STUDS TERKEL
THE STUDS TERKEL PROGRAM
1995

SACKS: *I'm writing this with my left hand, although I am strongly right-handed. I had surgery to my right shoulder a month ago and I'm not permitted, not capable of, use of the right arm at this time. I write slowly, awkwardly, but more easily, more naturally with each passing day. I am adapting, learning all the while. Not merely this left-handed writing, but a dozen other left-handed skills as well.*

TERKEL: That's Oliver Sacks reading a deceptively casual preface to his most recent book. Oliver Sacks is a wonder of a neurologist, who has the soul of a poet but the writing gifts of a fine novelist, as you know, having read his other works. His most recent book is called *An Anthropologist on Mars*, subtitled *Seven Paradoxical Tales*. You remember the movie *Awakenings* too, based upon his writing case histories of some Tourette's people. I won't use the word "victims" because that's something entirely different. Tourette's people, as well as autistic people too. And this most recent one, that opening tells me a lot about you, Oliver, why you are so remarkable in your reaching out to those who are your patients. You yourself speak of your own experience with something that could be a handicap becoming something of a new avenue, a new opening for you.

SACKS: Well, when I first found the arm immobilized, I was in big trouble because I am so strongly right-handed. My balance was off, but I was very intrigued to find how quickly things started to change, and even though now I've sort of got use of the right arm back completely, I've kept some of those left-handed skills, and so it did actually add something to my repertoire.

TERKEL: These "left-handed skills." Even "left-hand" can be a metaphor for hitherto untried skills, come into play because you had this accident.

SACKS: Oh, absolutely. I was challenged, and my nervous system was challenged in a way which it had never been before.

TERKEL: And so you have "seven paradoxical tales." And I suppose the operative word is "paradoxical," in which people who have certain symptoms of diseases, but *because* of that, they have developed—an *adaptation* is the word—they develop new kinds of skills they hadn't had before.

SACKS: Right, and sometimes, more deeply, they have become reorganized and sort of developed different centers almost to their lives.

TERKEL: Is it fair to say that you yourself, that you, Oliver Sacks, revealed some of your own vulnerabilities as you talked, you and the patient together? They recognize that don't they? That you're a fellow passenger.

SACKS: Yes. Yes, I think so. Perhaps I've changed. Originally, I used to think of myself as remote and detached and, you know, almost a sort of a godlike figure. But now I feel I'm quite as vulnerable as they are, and they can see that. And I think there's certainly a sort of sharing.

TERKEL: Let's start with the first tale, let's start with the colorblind painter. And he was a rather distinguished successful painter who was a master, by the way, of color. And you have some illustrations in the book.

SACKS: Well, I got a letter from him at the start of 1986, saying that he had had a car accident and a head injury three weeks before. He'd been stunned. He'd been briefly amnesic, but then he found that he had lost all his sense of color. And later he amplified the letter and he described to me how he had driven to his studio the following day. He knew it was a bright, sunny day, but everything looked gray and misty. The police stopped him for going past two red lights. He said he hadn't noticed them. His paintings were drained of color, and since color had been so important for him, they were drained of meaning as well. Then in a sort of panic he went home and he found his wife had been transformed, that she had become as he put it "an animated gray statue." And then as he looked at his own flesh, he shuddered at the grayness of *it*. He closed his eyes, trying to bring color back, but he found his imagination and his memory had been voided of color too. And so this was the story, and he wrote to me and said, *Can you understand? Can you help? What's happened?*

TERKEL: And it begins he lost color, which provided so much, if I may say so, *color* to his life. Suddenly everything is gray. The oranges are gray and dull and leaden and deadly. Now, we're in a quandary here, aren't we? Now what happens?

SACKS: Well, I saw him. He was very depressed then. He felt this was the end of him as an artist and as a man. Neurologically, the matter was *relatively* simple. You know, neurologists are employed to make diagnoses and fix things if they can. I tested him and it became evident that two small areas at the back of the brain, in the visual parts of the brain, had been knocked out. One needs these areas to construct color. You know, color isn't just given to us. Color has to be constructed by the brain from information which comes to it, and if that's knocked out, then you can no longer see color, or imagine it, or remember it, or dream it.

TERKEL: So here is an artist, a painter known for his color, but now, daily, something is happening, unexpected. He's developing something called a "night vision"—that darkness suddenly becomes in a sense *light* to him, as it would be dark to others. Or am I wrong about that?

SACKS: Well, I think something like this happened later. But at the time he came to me, he was conscious only of impoverishment, ugliness, horror, and a sort of nightmare vision. One could find that these two little areas had been knocked out.

I said I didn't know if there'd be any recovery, and I couldn't do anything to promote recovery, but I hoped that he might start to feel more at home, and at least cope with this black-and-white world.

TERKEL: Ah, now, wait. I forgot. I had eliminated *you* here! *You* now are seeing him, and you see the quandary he's in. And you yourself, by the way, writing this, you're just recovering from the loss of the right hand, temporarily, but you're developing something else with your left, and other aspects. So in a way, subconsciously, that might have been a way of work with you. Maybe he can—something else can happen to make up for his loss of color.

SACKS: Well, I hoped that this might be the case. What did happen was really rather dramatic. About four or five weeks after the injury, as he was driving to the studio one morning (although we hadn't done any work in that time), he saw the sunrise. He can't see red and the sunrise seemed smoky and dramatic and, as he said it, "apocalyptic." He thought it was like some huge nuclear explosion. He wondered if anyone had ever seen such a sunrise before, or the sun rise in such a way before. And he went back, and he did a very powerful black-and-white painting, which he called *Nuclear Sunrise*. And this for him was the beginning of a change.

TERKEL: Now that *Nuclear Sunrise*, which is stunning, and you have reproductions here, that *Nuclear Sunrise* that he did— that is apocalyptic, and stark, black and white—he could not have done had he not lost a sense of color. Or could he?

SACKS: Um, no. I think it did represent the beginnings of a new sort of sensibility for him. And now the world, which had lost its meaning and power with color, regained meaning and power, but in different terms. And he also felt that the sense of texture and movement was heightened. He felt that his night vision was heightened. He started to feel that he hadn't just lost something, but that something new and important was coming to him. And this charged up his painting and sensibility again.

TERKEL: As you say, so here is the thing: adaptation. And something new is developing that might not have been. And, even light, he saw light in a new *light*. You know I was thinking of something strange; I was thinking of Hopper—I don't know why.

SACKS: Yes, well, interestingly, I know another sort of totally colorblind person who loves Hopper's work more than any other.

TERKEL: Now, explain that. I said it because—

SACKS: Well it's, I mean, this is part of your clairvoyance. I think, of course, a lot of Hopper's paintings are night scenes—

TERKEL: Of course, *Nighthawks*! My case is personal because below the hotel where I was as a boy was an all-night restaurant, much like the diner in Hopper's. So night scenes and now we come to night don't we? To our friend Mr. I., this painter.

SACKS: Well, he started to become a night person, as he said. He didn't like the glare and brightness of the day. But he started exploring at night and he said he felt the equal of anyone else at night. And many of his paintings were nocturnal scenes. But one saw how the whole organization of his life changed.

TERKEL: And now we come to end—though there was much more to it, of course—this case history. It was a new world of seeing. Using your words, "a new world of seeing." He saw a new way, and so new forms! Forms! Explain the use of the Mondrian test.

SACKS: Oh, well, this is a complicated sort of thing. But sometimes one can use geometrical abstracts rather like the paintings of Mondrian to test color vision. You know the perception of color isn't just some simple, physical translation of wavelength, but it depends on making a survey of a whole scene, and this is tested with the Mondrians. One could show with this test, in fact, that this painter was receiving the wavelength information in his brain, but he couldn't connect it to construct color. And this, in fact, led to a suggestion by a colleague that it might be possible to train another part of his brain to construct color. And the painter's response to this was very interesting. He said, "If you had offered this to me at first," he said, "I would have loved you, you would have given me what I had lost back." He said, "Now I don't want it." He said, "Color has become meaningless." He said, "My world is reconstructed and it's complete and coherent and fine as it is—"

TERKEL: That's fantastic.

SACKS: "—and you keep color."

TERKEL: And he's doing it now—

SACKS: And he's doing it now.

TERKEL: Sans color.

SACKS: Right.

TERKEL: This is the first of Oliver Sacks's new book, *An Anthropologist on Mars*. We'll come to that very title itself. Alien place for this particular person, this woman, who is remarkable. And of course we'll come to "The Last Hippie," to the surgeon with Tourette's, to a special kind of artist who re-sees the hometown of his childhood landscape of his dreams, and an autistic kid who becomes a remarkable artist. But in every case, Oliver Sacks, you find this new avenue opening, that would not have opened had they not had that disease! That's the paradox.

SACKS: Right.

TERKEL: Well having Oliver Sacks as a guest is always a delight because it's exciting, but always that added element involving the human spirit, the body, befouled by disease in so many ways and yet overcoming it, and then a new something occurs, as in the case of, well, "The Last Hippie" is more of a wistful one. Well, describe "The Last Hippie."

SACKS: Well, this Greg was born in the '50s, and he was a hippie, part of the hippie generation in the '60s, and he was very musical. He was one of the first Dead Heads. He loved the Grateful Dead. But he also smoked pot and he took acid. He used to go down and listen to Allen Ginsberg declaiming in the village, and then he joined the Hare Krishna movement. And there things went wrong. He complained that he wasn't seeing properly, that something was happening with his vision, but this got interpreted spiritually as an inner light—

TERKEL: Bliss.

SACKS: —a state of bliss, and other symptoms also got misinterpreted and, really, in a very tragic way, he was allowed to develop a large brain tumor which blinded him and altered his personality. It pressed on the frontal lobes, and it pressed on the memory centers and the temporal lobes. When the tumor was removed—it was a benign tumor—the damage had been done. And so when he came into our hospital in '75, he was a young man with no future, in a sense, and with an amnesia which had marooned him in the 1960s. Because nothing new could be registered.

TERKEL: So things register with him: the '60s, even the songs of the Grateful Dead. Music now and then would pick him up. Rock 'n' roll, especially Grateful Dead. That would help him. There was a figure, almost clay-like, coming alive on hearing some of the music, for a moment.

SACKS: Well, for a moment, sometimes for minutes. I'm

fascinated by this power of music. I saw it in the *Awakenings* patients, and I've seen it in so many, and I experienced it myself when I was a patient.

TERKEL: Well, that, when you broke your leg, and you were in a cast, and you were laid up for a while. And if I remember right, a mountain climbing accident—

SACKS: Right.

TERKEL: *A Leg to Stand On.* It was Mozart and music that saved you.

SACKS: Yeah, I mean, in a sort of way I'd forgotten what was the use of the leg and what walking was like. And I think music sort of brought back the rhythms, but certainly with Greg, who would be blank and zombie-like for much of the time, he came alive completely with music, and at one point I wanted to sort of see him have more of a life. And when I heard the Grateful Dead was in town in '91—

TERKEL: You took him to Madison Square Garden.

SACKS: Right. And the first half of the concert was all early music. He knew it all. He loved it, no problems. Although he kept questioning me . . . he knew all the Grateful Dead people, but he kept asking where they were. I pointed them out, and he'd say, "Where's Pigpen?" And I said to him that he's not with them anymore. He said, "What happened? He got busted or something?" and I said, "No, no, Greg, he died."

And he said, "That's awful." And then thirty seconds later, he'd say, "Is that Pigpen there?"

TERKEL: So there's an Alzheimer's . . . kind of.

SACKS: Well, he's not Alzheimer-like. He's not demented, I think. Greg is very bright. But he's like an amnesic, like Jimmy the Last Mariner, whom I wrote about—

TERKEL: Yeah, I remember that, yeah.

SACKS: But certainly he knew everything of the first half—

TERKEL: So that's it. So everything went dead after the '60s. He knew all the '60s songs of the Grateful Dead but nothing new. So now we have to come back to you, Oliver Sacks, we can't leave you out of this. You took him to Madison Square Garden, and you sat with him there, and you become part of the lives of these people themselves. You are a fellow passenger on this journey. You are.

SACKS: Well, I think one needs to share the experience as much as possible. In the second half, Greg got very puzzled. He said, "It's *weird* stuff." He said, "It's like the music of the future," and that gave me a chill when he said that, because of course it is a future for him, which in a sense he can never know. But he was in a great mood coming back from the concert and he said, "I'll never forget it; it's been wonderful."

TERKEL: There was a great moment. Now did he forget it?

SACKS: Well, the next morning, I went up to the ward and he was looking a bit blank. But I brought up the subject, I crossed my fingers, I said, you know, "What about the Grateful Dead?" And he said, "Oh, they're a great group, I heard them in Central Park, I heard them in Fillmore East." And I said, "Yeah, but, um, have you heard them lately? Have you heard them in Madison Square Garden?" And he said, "No." He said, "I've never been to the garden."

TERKEL: And that was the night before, he was there.

SACKS: And yet, and this is my footnote to the end of the piece, the interesting thing was he remembered some of the new music, even though he didn't know where he had heard it. And I think musical memory may have somewhat different mechanisms—

TERKEL: Musical memory, before we go to the third life, the surgeon with Tourette's, a remarkable Canadian figure for that musical memory. I remember there was talk about—I forgot, it was years ago—it was in Hungary and some old women . . . No, old women *came* to America, and they had lost their memory and all, but someone played Hungarian folk music as collected by Bartok and Kodaly, and they heard the Hungarian folk songs of their young girlhood, and suddenly they came alive!

SACKS: Oh, absolutely, one sees this again and again. And you mentioned Alzheimer's disease, but I think with people who have often become disorganized, and very lost through

Alzheimer's disease, music from their youth or familiar music will suddenly recall them to themselves and to their former worlds, and even the EEGs get better. Neurologically, they can be much better for a few minutes, and I think, you know, the music has a great power.

TERKEL: Oliver Sacks, *An Anthropologist on Mars*. We spoke of a surgeon, remarkable, in Canada, named Bennett, and he's got Tourette's. Just a word about Tourette's, for those who may not know, you were the first, well, Tourette's was known, but you were the first one to make it known to the great many of us through an earlier of your books, *The Man Who Mistook His Wife for a Hat*, and some of the earlier stories. Tourette's involves tics of various sorts and—

SACKS: And all sorts of convulsive movements and noises and sometimes thoughts as well, and people who have it seem sort of accelerated and sudden. And this was certainly so with this man Bennett whom I had seen at a meeting actually in Boston, and some of his tics were very extraordinary. One of them consisted of suddenly putting his foot on top of people's heads. It was a very, very agile, and one somehow felt *affectionate*, tic.

TERKEL: He was a highly respected surgeon, lecturing to some of the young medical students. But as he's lecturing—it's funny, by the way, you don't mind. And I imagine Tourette's people wouldn't mind too much, if people laughed too, because they know sometimes what they do is funny.

SACKS: Yes.

TERKEL: Don't they?

SACKS: Oh, oh, absolutely.

TERKEL: Yeah. And so what he's doing is he's kicking his feet in the air, I think, as he's lecturing and, the students are listening, deadpan, seriously, to his very excellent lectures . . . as he's kicking his feet!

SACKS: Well, when he told me he was a teacher and a surgeon, I couldn't believe it, but then, as you say, when I visited him in Canada, I saw him talking with his colleagues, sort of lying on his back, sort of kicking his foot in the air. And, you know, but with a sort of perfectly composed discourse.

TERKEL: So there's a split here. He is able to concentrate so much on his work as a surgeon that the Tourette's Syndrome tics all disappear, don't they? At that moment, when he's doing that operation.

SACKS: Well, I scrubbed with him for a long operation, it was two and a half hours, and there was no hint of Tourette's in it, and he wasn't controlling it. There was just no impulse to tic at that time, and all his whole mind, he said he just was thinking of his work and thinking of the operation. And one can see this in other ways, sometimes with Tourettic artists or musicians, that when they're in the mode of art or whatever, they may not have any tics.

TERKEL: Well one of your patients earlier, in an earlier work, you describe this guy who, on weekends, was a great jazz drummer and he had wild Tourette's symptoms. Explain that. What happened.

SACKS: Well, you know, this is the man I call Witty Ticcy Ray in the *Hat* book. Well, in his excited state, he was a very good jazz drummer. He might suddenly convulsively hit the drums and then very rapidly he would improvise on this and he was famous for these improvisations which were actually partly—

TERKEL: Well, he had Tourette's!

SACKS: Partly Tourettic, yeah, and when he was on medication to tamp things down, in fact, he lost the ability to improvise, or even play decently.

TERKEL: So, when he lost the Tourette's symptoms with the medication, he could be whatever he was, a good accountant or something. I don't mean to put down accountants, but I mean that, well, a great jazz drummer with Tourette's!

SACKS: And, you know, with Bennett the surgeon, I don't know whether he lost his Tourette's when he was operating, or whether, as it were, the Tourettic energy was somehow cohered into a creative—

TERKEL: Is it fair to say, I may be jumping, may be assuming, that Tourette's is really a symptom of . . . creative people? Not all are, but there's a creative aspect. Or is that assuming too much?

SACKS: Well, no, anyone can have Tourette's. You can be a genius, you can be a moron, it sort of makes no distinctions. But it does have a sort of energy of its own. Indeed, there's been a recent book about Tourette's called *A Mind of Its Own*. And something like Tourette's, with its sort of strange energy, and its swerves and its fancies, I think can connect with the mind, and if it's present with the creativity of the person, to produce an intriguing sort of compound.

TERKEL: So the word here you brought up, the word "energy"—there's an *energy* here. As you were describing a woman—this might again be from the *Hat* book, or *The Man Who Mistook His Wife for a Hat*—this woman who has Tourette's, somewhere along Forty-second Street, goes into the alley and starts mimicking all the passersby. They recognize themselves! She's so good that they're furious.

SACKS: Although, although this wasn't a *conscious* mimicry: it was a sort of convulsive taking in of other people's gestures and faces, even in split seconds. But, no, there's a huge energy in Tourette's. And it can tear people apart, it can be very disabling, but it can also be focused in a very positive way.

TERKEL: So, this is Dr. Bennett, then, and the operations. And he's highly respected, and as you leave him, you're with him of course, he has you wash up with him and watch the operation. In another case, you take part in some adventures with some of your patients, so he flies a plane, an airplane, Dr. Bennett, the Tourette's guy, and you're his passenger.

SACKS: Yeah, I was a bit taken aback. I thought I was just going to take a commercial airline back to Calgary and he suddenly said that he'd fly me in his little plane. He said, "I'm the world's only flying Tourettic surgeon!" And I was a bit alarmed. But he did have sort of little tics in the plane—he would sort of touch his eyes, his nose, the cockpit—I kept having fantasies that he would have *big* tics and sort of spin the plane or loop the loop or he'd suddenly leap out and touch the propeller. And, you know, people with Tourette's are often fascinated by spinning objects and they like sometimes playing with danger or playing with boundaries. But in fact none of this happened and he was a superb pilot, as he was a superb surgeon.

TERKEL: So as you left him last, he's a surgeon with Tourette's. Simple as that.

SACKS: Right. And you know after I'd originally written the piece, five more surgeons with Tourette's came out of the closet as well as some other medical men, and I think, Studs, you told me that you yourself had once known a psychiatrist—

TERKEL: This guy who was a remarkably very well-respected one, but he would bark like a dog. He barked continuously, in the middle of conversations, and you'd hear that sound: *WOMP!* But when he got up to lecture, and I heard him a couple of times, just like Dr. Bennett: he was remarkable. Easy, cool, controlled, eloquent. Not a bark, you know. And so there was that aspect. So adaptation or . . . what? I guess the word is "concentration" on what you're doing at that moment.

SACKS: I don't know what happens, but whatever it is I think the whole sort of, you know, nervous system is reconfigured.

TERKEL: We're talking to Oliver Sacks. You realize, like with Joe Louis, there's more where that came from. Always, it seems, because your books continue with your stories, your case histories, that of course are theatrical and not accidentally so. Many of your works have been adapted. *The Man Who Mistook His Wife for a Hat*: *The Man Who*, now a play enthusiastically received in New York, directed by Peter Brooke, also to become the basis of an opera.

SACKS: Right, yeah.

TERKEL: And then the movie in which Robin Williams played you. Was that a pretty good interpretation of yourself?

SACKS: It was disconcertingly close at times!

TERKEL: But it's true though, that your work then is by the very nature theatrical, isn't it? Because what we're describing is theater.

SACKS: Yeah, I know. I think there is a sort of *living* theater when, you know, in the clinical life people open themselves, they tell you these stories of how life has, you know, how a strange sort of neurology has wounded them, or pushed them in various ways and their responses. But I think there's a sort of *bad* theater, I think it would be awful to portray people as a sort of freak show. But I think with respect, one can convey the drama.

TERKEL: But also to me it's overcoming. The idea that you *overcome*. I don't mean a sentimental overcome. I mean the fact that you, again, and that surgery on your right hand, and your left gets to work. You know, you see, the right hand is the doer, the left hand is the dreamer. Some of the jazzmen say. And so, the dream! So how to describe you? You're a neurologist, yet you know you're a wonderful writer. But you're also a chronicler, and, in fact, there's a poetic touch. But it can't be helped—that's what you are, and that's the work you do. And so there is this artist. His name is Magnani.

SACKS: Franco!

TERKEL: Franco Magnani.

SACKS: Here again it was sort of a happy accident that we met. The museum in San Francisco, the Exploratorium, had an exhibit on memory, and he was billed as "The Memory Artist." They had fifty of his paintings there, of the little village where he'd been born in Italy, Pontito, and, next to these, photos taken by the Exploratorium's photographer in exactly the same places, wherever possible, as the paintings were done from. Now the resemblance was uncanny. But Franco had not seen his village for thirty years or more, and this in fact was entirely the village as it was before he was nine years old. And so he was somehow retrieving apparently very, very, early memories, and was haunted and obsessed by them, but putting them down very accurately. And this whole business struck me as very strange. I wanted to learn more about it.

TERKEL: It's a *Remembrance of Things Past*, as Proust does, but there's something else here. It's not inward, as you point out; it's outward.

SACKS: Well, I found myself wondering whether he was a sort of visual Proust. Although there were no events and no people in his paintings, it was just the stones and the masonry. Almost like a stage set. This strange sort of motionless Pontito, ready to be populated, but never actually populated. But things had come on him suddenly, actually, when he was in his early thirties when he decided to start life in America. And then he had an illness, and he had a high fever, seizures, convulsions, and strange dreams in which he would dream of Pontito every night. And when he woke in the morning, these dreams were solid like three dimensional hallucinations or visions in front of him, and though he'd never drawn before, he felt he could take a pen and trace the outlines. Now, I think it's very odd and complex. I think Franco has a sort of epilepsy, as it were, an epilepsy of memory.

TERKEL: An epilepsy of memory because it takes a jump, sudden starts. You say he had details, almost photographic, and yet it's not. And yet, for example, I'm looking at one right now of his, it looks like a Magritte for some reason. It's not real! It's *dreamlike*.

SACKS: Well these, I think, seizures, which used to be described as literal memories, also have all sorts of dreamlike qualities. And certainly he himself, if he has an organic malady here, a strange sort of epilepsy, he's certainly using it in a way both obsessive and creative to recreate a vision of this village.

TERKEL: You know, it's funny, throughout these tales, a creativity appears, except perhaps in the case of the lost, "The Last Hippie." But in almost every other case the creativity comes out of the disease.

SACKS: Here again with temporal lobe epilepsy, in a strange way, this can sometimes incline people in a sort of mystical direction, or can incline them to verbosity, or compulsive drawing. It can sometimes ruin a life, as Tourette's can, but also, sometimes, it can be held together in a creative way and heighten the life, which I think it's certainly done with Franco, although it's complex because his life is also impoverished in the present, because his mind is a result from the past.

TERKEL: A paradoxical tale. We haven't come to autism. "Autism" immediately is a frightening word, as it is a frightening, uh . . . burden. We know young people of autism and a couple of people in it who are remarkable; not *though* autistic, but autistic *and* remarkable. I would start with Stephen Wiltshire, a West Indian kid of thirteen, fourteen. The artist, the painter.

SACKS: Well, again, I first heard of Stephen because a publisher sent me some of his drawings, along with some history of him. And I was staggered by these exquisite drawings of

London, and puzzled. When I was next in London, I spoke to
my brother, who was a physician there, and strangely he said,
"Stephen?" He says, "He's a patient of mine!"

TERKEL: He was your brother's patient! You come from a
family of medical people, neurologists.

SACKS: And so my brother David filled me in with the early
history that Stephen had been manifestly autistic at the age
of two, rocking and screaming. Everything had become
much worse with the death of his father when he was three.
He was sent to a special school, but he was really regarded
as hopeless and ineducable. And then when he was six, a
teacher had discovered him doing exquisite tiny drawings of
the Tower of London, and the Houses of Parliament. And
Stephen hadn't gone through any of the usual stages of doo-
dling and drawings, which other children do, just suddenly
with these exquisite drawings. And very rapidly, these won
an exhibit, they were sent in. And so when I heard about
things, Stephen had become nationally famous in England,
there'd been a television program, and he was about to have
a book published. So, he was certainly a prodigy, an autistic
and retarded boy, with a so-called savant gift for drawing.
And I was very curious to meet him. And I got a chance to do
so for the first time the following year when he came to New
York. At that time, his language was very poor. He would
nod his head and smile and he had a few words. We went
outside. He glanced at my house, and then he went back and
did a beautiful little drawing of it. Actually, I felt he could

have done the entire street. I think in that single, indifferent but all-comprehensive glance, I think he'd taken in the whole street. I was puzzled. On the one hand, one couldn't interrupt him, there was a tremendous sort of concentration, in a sense, and then, in another way, he seemed to be looking around and whistling and listening to a tape recorder. So it was as if only a part of him was doing this drawing, and the rest of him sort of seemed unconnected.

TERKEL: So it was concentration on the drawing, but his ability was such that even though he may not have been fully concentrating on it, because there were distractions, he would come through with remarkable works, like one he was doing a take off on Matisse. But the fact that you have illustrations here. This is Matisse! I mean he caught the *spirit*, or what you called "Matisseness." He could not simply read, was not simply imitating. It's more than that.

SACKS: Well, I'm not sure what it is. And, incidentally, I know of one autistic artist who became a great menace as a forger. He is now employed in one of the great auction houses. And he's very good at telling other people's forgeries.

TERKEL: Really? This is interesting, so this guy became . . . A creative autist can go two ways: I can't do well, can dupe people good, and dupe people *good*.

SACKS: Absolutely. Well, Stephen seems able to catch anything, whether it's a Matisse, whether it's the Grand Canyon,

whether it's a cathedral, or whether it's an elephant. And, you
know, so brilliantly, I mean his drawings are quite wonderful
and they brought joy to millions of people.

TERKEL: You know, I'm thinking of one Dr. Bettelheim, head
of the Orthogenic School in Chicago, in *The Empty Fortress*,
his book, he speaks of Joey the Mechanical Boy. And Joey
the Mechanical Boy was so good, he was an autistic, that
people would, there were no wires, but he said there were
wires, and he acted as though there actually were all kinds of
wires. People, visitors would step over the imaginary wires
or walk around, because they believed Joey. So, one day Dr.
Bettelheim asked if he could come to WFMT studios, he's
interested in being a radio engineer. And I met him. And
he is quite remarkable. I couldn't tell one thing or another, he
seemed quite normal. He was Joey the Mechanical Boy and
learning things from our engineer listening and I think he became a sound engineer somewhere else. But it's that constant,
but it's making *others* believe it's actually so.

SACKS: Well, a good number, something like at least ten percent, and sometimes I think it may be much more than that,
of autistic people have these strange gifts and concentrations,
sometimes visual, sometimes musical, Stephen was very musical as well, although sometimes these seem to be unconnected
with, you know, with personality or the mind as a whole. Very
isolated, strange gifts, but of a prodigious order.

TERKEL: So we have these strengths. I don't mean to be Polly-
anna, not this tragic stuff. But we have these *strengths* that

come through as a result of the disease. What is it, you're quoting the celebrated Osler here at the beginning in one of your epigraphs. What is it you say? "Ask not what disease the person has, rather what person the disease has." You were about to say . . .

SACKS: Well, it's never just the disease, there's always this conjunction. So, how much has autism brought to Stephen, but how much has Stephen brought to autism.

TERKEL: Oliver Sacks. This recent book is called *An Anthropologist on Mars: Seven Paradoxical Tales*, and it's almost a continuation of all your others. But more and more and more we find out about this crazy thing called the human, what, psyche, but *possibilities* within that which is definitely a disease.

SACKS: Right. And the different ways in which people can make their worlds and how paradoxically disease can almost force one to make another world in a different sort of world.

TERKEL: And so with Oliver Sacks, it's amazing how quickly I feel I'd do another hour with you but we shall meet him again and again and again. And certainly, when your play based upon *The Man Who*, it's called *The Man Who*, will be coming to Chicago. Perhaps you will be here with your next book too. And also your book on the world of the deaf. What is it called again?

SACKS: *Seeing Voices.*

TERKEL: *Seeing Voices.* And then, just to name some of the books, of course. *Migraine*, that's one of your earliest ones. *Awakenings*, of course we know, *A Leg to Stand On*—your own adventure, *The Man Who Mistook His Wife for a Hat.* And then the new one called—this one—*An Anthropologist on Mars.*

OLIVER SACKS ON EMPATHY AS A PATH TO INSIGHT

INTERVIEW WITH LISA BURRELL
HARVARD BUSINESS REVIEW
NOVEMBER 2010

BURRELL: Dr. Sacks, what made you decide to go into neurology, besides being born into a family of doctors?

SACKS: Well, both my parents in fact trained in neurology, but I think the important thing was that the brain seemed to me by far the most interesting thing in the world. I am full of admiration for kidneys and kidney specialists, but the brain is much more interesting than a kidney. And the brain both shapes us and is shaped by us. And the brain is who we are.

BURRELL: Your new book, *The Mind's Eye*, is largely about how the brain adapts when seeing is compromised. Can you talk a bit about that?

SACKS: Well, as a physician or scientist interested in the nervous system and in patients, I learn by seeing what happens when things go wrong. It's very difficult to learn when everything goes right. You think, for example, the whole world, full of color, and movement, and depth, and meaning, is given to you. But it's not. It is dependent on the goodwill and the good functioning of forty or fifty different parts of the brain, all linked together. And any one of these can go wrong and knock out a single thing, like knocking out color but nothing else.

BURRELL: Your case histories illustrate some debilitating losses.

SACKS: Yes. One of them was about a writer who suddenly lost the ability to read. First he naturally experienced this as an absolute catastrophe. I mean, what worse could happen to a writer? But then various things came to his aid. And in a mysterious way, he thought he was improving, that he was gaining the normal visual ability to read back. But he wasn't. What was happening was that he was unconsciously copying the shapes of letters with his tongue. And that would show people who lose their reading are still able to write, which is a strange thing. So in a way, he was converting what his eyes saw and writing it with his tongue. And I would absolutely not have thought such a thing was possible.

And another one of the pieces is about face blindness, which is surprisingly common and sometimes crippling. Sometimes there are people who may not recognize their children, or they may not recognize themselves in a mirror. This sounds silly and funny, and comic situations can arise from it. I've had a few of them myself, because I am moderately face blind. But when people are severely face blind, it's quite an affliction. But it was hardly described medically, and hardly described in the public sphere either.

BURRELL: How common is it?

SACKS: Well, I think it probably affects 2 percent or 2.5 percent of the population, whatever that is. Six million people. And so one of the reasons for writing about that is to try and bring that to public awareness. Most of the pieces in this book were conceived before I had my own visual problems. They weren't prompted by my visual problems. I've been interested in vision as long as I can remember.

BURRELL: Can you talk a bit about the role of empathy in your writing?

SACKS: Well, I think it's absolutely crucial. And if for some reason the empathy is not there—I have never written about anyone I disliked, or for that matter, anyone I couldn't feel my way into to some extent.

BURRELL: That's the first rule of writing fiction, too. You want people to identify with your characters.

SACKS: Yes. Well, I certainly find that. I know, for example, when I published *The Man Who Mistook His Wife for a Hat*, one of the pieces was called "The Lost Mariner," Jimmy. And I literally got hundreds of letters saying, "How is Jimmy? Say hello to him from me." And it was really quite extraordinary.

BURRELL: How can people with neurological disorders shape their work environments to accommodate their symptoms?

SACKS: Ooh. That's a big question. I was just at a writing colony up in the Adirondacks, and I read a bit of my piece on face blindness. And I was then told a rather painful story—both painful and funny—which was that the year before, one of the residents had so liked the place that she wanted to join the staff. But it turned out that she was so face blind that she couldn't reliably recognize any of the other people on the staff, or any of the people there. And they had to let her go.

But one has to try and shape the environment. My first story in *The Mind's Eye* is about a woman, a very gifted musician, who actually becomes unable to recognize anything visually in the ordinary way. And yet she has completely organized her own apartment in terms of color, size, position, context. And so she has adapted the apartment to herself, and very successfully.

BURRELL: Has your own struggle with ocular cancer changed the way you work and think as a doctor?

SACKS: I think it didn't change it essentially. It may have deepened it. We all know that we're going to die sometime, that human beings are mortal, that life has a limited span, even if one is a sea anemone. Actually, that's not so if one is a sea anemone. Some sea anemones are three hundred years old and going strong. But when you have something like this, you know it's there, that it's not completely removed. And I think it's given me a paradoxical feeling of how precious life is, and how precious time is. And not to waste it. I do speak more easily to other people with cancers and things, because I can speak as one of them.

BURRELL: Sure.

SACKS: I think one needs to have some sort of inner vision as well. When I was thinking and writing about people who are deaf, and born deaf, I had a friend—actually a hearing child of deaf parents, extremely fluent in both sign language and speech—who would often come along with me. When I went to the island of the colorblind, which I wrote about in another book, one of my fellow travelers was a physiologist who himself was born totally colorblind. In this way, there can be no condescension or looking at a distance. But now my own cancer is a sort of mediator. Some of my patients at least know that I too am a patient. Although in some sense, we're all patients.

THE JOY OF AGING

INTERVIEW WITH TOM ASHBROOK
ON POINT
JULY 18, 2013

ASHBROOK: Oliver Sacks, thank you very much for joining us today and happy birthday, sir.

SACKS: Thank you, Tom. It's a pleasure to be with you.

ASHBROOK: You make eighty sound like it's just a big party. Is it really?

SACKS: Well, I had a lot of parties last week, now the parties are over and real life begins.

ASHBROOK: How's it compare to what you anticipated, when you were, I don't know, thirty or forty or fifty, and looking forward to eighty?

SACKS: Well, I don't think I thought too much about being older. Although of course, I saw all of my relatives and teachers getting older. I'm a little startled at finding myself eighty, as if it happened suddenly.

ASHBROOK: What's so good about it?

SACKS: Well, first, various pressures are diminished. I have a feeling of leisure and freedom and being able to do what I want, and being able to do what I want includes continuing to work. And as you said, there are long perspectives. I've seen a lot, I've been through a lot, good and bad, I've seen governments rise and fall and scientific theories rise and fall, and I think there's a breadth of mind which, provided the brain is healthy, comes with age.

ASHBROOK: So, I don't know if this is possible, if memory is strong enough, but compare a great day or a great frame of mind when you were, you name it, thirty or forty or fifty, compared to a great day and a great frame of mind now that you're eighty. Are they the same thing or is there a qualitative difference to "the joy of old age," as you put it?

SACKS: Well, on my fortieth birthday I went for a long swim. And on my eightieth birthday I went for a long swim.

ASHBROOK: That's good!

SACKS: So, so, I certainly enjoyed them both. But I think things have a quieter tone at eighty, but that doesn't mean they're less intense, they are simply less flamboyant.

ASHBROOK: You're not in denial about where eighty puts you on the spectrum here. You write that sometimes you just burst out, "I'm glad I'm not dead!"

SACKS: Yeah, um, absolutely. When the weather is beautiful,

I feel that. And of course, a third of my contemporaries *are* dead. And another large fraction of them have dementias or physical problems and don't have much to look forward to.

ASHBROOK: I mean, you tell this wonderful story, I guess it all depends what frame of mind you bring to it, of Samuel Beckett in Paris with a friend of yours, and your friend saying to him, "Doesn't a day like this make you glad to be alive?" and Beckett answered . . .

SACKS: "I wouldn't go as far as that."

ASHBROOK: So, is this just your natural chemistry to be inclined toward happiness? Joy? And Beckett's maybe, you know, a bit more sour?

SACKS: I'm not sure why my natural happiness does [exist]. I'm not one of the blue-eyed, optimistic people whom William James speaks about. But there is a lot that I am very grateful for and to be happy about. I've been lucky enough to be in good health, and to have friends and students. I love my work, and I love writing, and for the moment, I'm still able to go sort of on all cylinders with both of these.

ASHBROOK: I mean, it's not as though you've been spared all the afflictions of, you know, you've got your joint issues, your vision issues, it's not like everything's running perfectly, and yet you have this sense of fulfillment, of happiness. Where do you find it most deeply now?

SACKS: I think I probably find it in work. And in the feeling that I've encompassed much more in the way of knowledge about the brain and about people and in a sense about the universe than I had at sixty or forty. There's a good feeling of fullness and less a feeling of incompleteness. I don't know that I ever had a strong fear of death, and I don't have it now, but I used to have all sorts of regrets for what I hadn't done, and now many of the things I hadn't done I have done, and life has been kind that way.

ASHBROOK: What kind of reaction have you had to your op-ed piece? I'm sure many people read it with great interest. Everyone thinks, you know, sooner or later, about age, and many people are staring straight at it or in it. How do people respond to your headline, "The Joy of Old Age"?

SACKS: Well, first, that wasn't my headline. That was the *Times*'s. My title was just "On Turning Eighty." I didn't expect this piece; it happened rather suddenly. I mentioned to a friend of mine that I'd had an odd dream about globules of mercury, rising up and down. Mercury—my boyhood was full of chemistry and atomic numbers—mercury is element eighty. And somehow that dream started me off and I wrote the piece in an hour or so and sent it off. But there have been different reactions. I think a majority of people who have anticipated decline, and going down, and losing it—in all sorts of ways, including losing the people they love, their contemporaries—have been somewhat encouraged by the piece. Some people have said, "Well, you're just lucky, and you can't speak for all of us." Some other people have gotten rather annoyed when I said that I had no wish for any postmortem existence or any interest in that. They say, "Don't you long for heaven?" And I say, "No, I'm happy with life on this planet," which, which will come to an end.

ASHBROOK: Maybe, I wonder about the range of responses, the range of experiences. You say work is important, and we can imagine that, but there *you* are, Oliver Sacks, lucky to have a very celebrated career that you can still exercise. Um, a sense of the fullness of life, of fulfillment. I mean, between your books and your life, Robin Williams played *you* in *Awakenings*. I mean, Bill Murray sort of played you in *The Royal Tenenbaums*. Talk about, this is not just an invisible, sad, little life. Maybe it's because you're sitting, at this point, on eighty years of this quite noted accomplishment that you're joyful.

SACKS: Well, that may be in part, but I've had many relatives who, who haven't perhaps had quite such a life, and they also enjoy eighty. My father who was a general practitioner, a physician in London, was going to retire at eighty but after forty-eight hours he came back. He later said he thought the eighties were one of the most enjoyable decades in his life and that he had more sense of leisure, even though he spent all day doing house calls and seeing his patients. At ninety, we said "Pop, at least stop doing house calls," and he said, "I'll stay with house calls, and I'll stop everything else." But he enjoyed every day, I think, more intensely and perhaps more consciously when he was eighty. because one doesn't know what lies ahead. Whether it will be a disease, or accident, or stroke, whatever, and so he loved going to concerts. He went to more concerts after he was eighty. And he traveled more. He loved the eighties.

ASHBROOK: Maybe younger people look a little frantic to you now, in all their urgent pursuits?

SACKS: Um, well, absolutely. This is sometimes the case. And certainly I'm not, you know, tormented by ambition or anxieties as much as I used to be.

ASHBROOK: What about those who aren't around anymore? What about missing them?

SACKS: Oh, um, intensely. My mother died forty years ago, my father died twenty-five years ago, but I still miss them deeply, and recently I've been able to find a treasure trove of letters between my parents and myself dating back to the early '60s when I came to America. And these have made me laugh and they've made me cry. And, it's, um, I do miss people intensely. But also, I meet new people.

ASHBROOK: Oliver Sacks, back in the day, you were a big-time weightlifter! I think you lifted six hundred pounds once, taking the prize in California. You must have been some specimen, what about the physical falling-aparts? The replaced knees and all the rest?

SACKS: Well, I certainly have replaced knees and all the rest. On one occasion, I was visited by a fellow weightlifter—he'd had a medal in the Olympics—and we looked at each other at said, "What fools we were."

ASHBROOK: Meaning?

SACKS: Meaning the body can't quite take that, such extreme exercise. You may be strong enough, but the ligaments and the tendons and so forth, and the discs, will break down. But still I was very happy to do it when I was thirty. Actually, I was twenty-eight. I got that Californian record.

ASHBROOK: Six hundred pounds! That's incredible! So now, I've seen the laundry list, and everybody's got one at a certain age. Are you self-pitying about those physical impediments or do they matter as much anymore?

SACKS: Um, I had a cancer. Melanoma in my eye. Which was irradiated. That eye now has no vision, but the cancer hasn't recurred. I sort of said to the cancer, "You can have the eye, but leave me alone." And so far, this is what the cancer has done. My balance is a bit bad, and when I'm outside, especially with crowds rushing around, I use a stick. And I don't drive because my vision's somewhat bad. On the other hand, I can read—though I use a magnifying glass—I can write up a storm, and I can swim up a storm. I love swimming and I feel young and strong, or *ageless* in the water. I think swimming is one of the few activities one can do for the first century.

ASHBROOK: Thank heavens for the first century! Thank heavens for water. I'm trying to think what sets you apart . . . I noted here, reading in your background, you've been in psychoanalysis for forty-six years with the same Freudian psychoanalyst. Is that key to your mental health? To the joy you find at eighty?

SACKS: Well he's not at all a doctrinaire, but he certainly knows me very well, and I think he likes me, which helps me like myself, which I haven't always done. And again, I think I'm lucky there, and more than lucky. I have had a lot of impulsive and destructive trades with drugs, and other ways, and my friends didn't expect me to make thirty, let alone forty, and I think it's partly due to the good analyst that I've actually reached eighty.

ASHBROOK: As a reporter out in the world, some years ago, I spoke with the oldest man in the world, or at least that was the claim—a hundred and twenty. He lived on a little island way down south of Japan, down toward what China and Japan are feuding about now, a tiny island. And of course you have to ask, you know, what's the secret of your long life. He said that he thought it was that he had not even left this tiny island until he was forty. He hadn't married until he was fifty. He had just done everything *late*. I thought of that as I read your piece. You were, in earlier decades of your life, Oliver Sacks, you were, forgive me, but I think everybody says, sort of, and you say, that you were morbidly shy, you were kind of a late bloomer. Could that be related to your happiness now?

SACKS: No, well, I think the shyness is more an affliction than anything else. But there's something to be said for late

blooming, because late blooming may be part of a contin-
ued blooming. There's something like music or mathematics,
when one starts very early, but where experience of life is concerned, I think it has to be relatively late. By the way, I once
saw an interview with the two oldest *women* in the world,
though they were only one hundred and fourteen. When they
were asked what contributed, the one in Holland said "herring," she had herring everyday, and the one in Texas said,
"minding my own business."

ASHBROOK: Herring and minding your own business! Herring everyday, my grandfather should've lived longer if that's
the secret. Oliver Sacks is with us. He turned eighty last week,
and it's pretty darn good, he says.

DR. SACKS LOOKS BACK

INTERVIEW WITH ROBERT KRULWICH
RECORDED LIVE AT THE BROOKLYN ACADEMY OF MUSIC
MAY 5, 2015

So we want to finish the night with a salute to a guy who's been on our program and part of our family pretty much from the beginning. I have known him for more than thirty-five years. Early on, when Radiolab *started, I asked him if he'd help us out and send us a few story ideas. He didn't send us a few, he sent us* bushels, *tales of chemistry and medicine, hallucinations, music, people—so many extraordinary people that he knew or found or helped, because the guy just doesn't run out. Dr. Oliver Sacks, neurologist, author, is a guy who notices everything. He's deeply interested in everything that happens around him and to him. And tonight, we're bringing him back on tape for what, alas, may be his final offering for us. As many of you know, Dr. Sacks recently was diagnosed with liver cancer, and he wrote about this in* The New York Times. *He said he plans to spend the time that he has left writing, being with friends, not doing interviews. But he did agree to share his thoughts exclusively with us tonight, for you gathered here, because he's one of our family. So, as I've done for decades now,*

I went over to his house in Manhattan with my mic, and I said to him . . .

KRULWICH: I just need to know, like, what just happened. A month and a half ago, you were fine . . . and then what?

SACKS: Um, at the beginning of the year I was fine. On the third of January, I felt a little queer and I passed some dark urine. I thought I had a little gallbladder attack and, um, didn't pay that much attention, but thought I better get things checked. And, um, the X-ray, which was expected only to show a couple of gallstones, showed hundreds of cysts in my liver. Although my doctor said he didn't know what these were, and I would need further tests, I knew what they were. I said, "It's happened."

And he was right. The doctors eventually confirmed that a cancer that had been found in his eye nine years ago had spread to his liver.

KRULWICH: Were you . . . frightened? Or relieved? Or concerned—or what?

SACKS: No, I, um, I think my first feeling was one of overwhelming sadness. Um, there are all sorts of things I won't see, um, and I won't do. One or two people have written to me, you know, consoling me, and said, "Well, you know, we all die." But fuck it! It's not like, *We all die.* It's like, *You have four months.*

KRULWICH: Has that, has your prog—what is your prognosis at this moment? Because I know you had an—

SACKS: Well, it gets revised.

It depends, of course, on how the cancer responds to treatments, or how quickly it spreads.

SACKS: So far, um, the metastases from my eye are only in my liver. I'm told they *love* liver. Actually, I love liver as well. And one of the magical things I did was to go and have liver and onions soon after.

KRULWICH: After this?

SACKS: [*laughing*] Yes.

KRULWICH: Oh, wow.

SACKS: And thinking, *That liver looks better than mine, probably.*

See, this is what he's like! Instead of being frightened by the thing that's trying to kill him, he's thinking about loving liver, and liver-lovers, and looking for connections, and wondering, and he doesn't stop. Case in point: A few months ago, his doctor said to him, "We're going to run a line up your liver, and, in effect, we're going to try to shave off or starve some of the cancer cells, first on one side and then on the other, to see if we can give you a little more time." But they warned him:

SACKS: As the metastases die, they put out various unpleasant chemicals.

That may exhaust you, tax your system badly.

SACKS: And, um, at one point . . .

Shortly after the procedures.

SACKS: I started talking a little strangely. And, um, as I was talking, I was also writing. Um, you will be the first person to see this.

So, he showed me a notebook, and we're showing it to you in just a moment, and you can see there's sort of writing there on the left. He's writing a book, actually a children's book about the elementary table, but, as he was writing, if you look to the next page, if you can see that, it gets a little bit wobbly? The letters.

SACKS: And then, there was some crossing out there.

KRULWICH: Yes, I see some crossing out.

SACKS: And then, rather dramatically, the writing changes.

KRULWICH: It actually, there's a large slash across it? And then it seems a little incoherent at the bottom?

SACKS: Yes, okay.

KRULWICH: And then it turns to pure . . . scribble.

SACKS: That is delirium. It crept up on me. All of this happened in the course of ten minutes.

You see what he's doing here, he's figuring out, "Okay, I'm writing at a constant speed, I know pretty much how fast I write, and so I can time this out. I can figure out exactly how long it took me to slip into *delirium and then* out *of this delirium." And he's doing this as a very, very sick man. It's science all the time!*

SACKS: I had to write it all out in a more medical way. I think this would form a lovely illustration. You put in a timeline of delirium, just coming like that.

KRULWICH: Why aren't you more frightened? Like, unusual! For any doctor and a man of science, you don't seem to worry at all when things become incoherent or strange. You're now showing it to me as if like, "Ooh, how interesting! I was crazy here for a little bit."

SACKS: Yeah, well . . .

The truth is, Oliver is fascinated by what goes on in the human mind, no matter how strange it gets up there. And one time, when he was a young resident in California driving his bike—and, by the way, I should show you what he looked like back then, when he was driving his bike. This I think is him in

New York, a kind of a, you know, oh-ho-ho. In the '60s, he was also a champion weightlifter, they called him Dr. Squat. And in this picture that we're showing you here, that's him raising six hundred pounds in order to win a trophy. Like, this is a—he was a champ. And you can see more pictures like these because we have signed copies of Oliver's new memoir out for sale in the lobby (it's a pretty good book too, by the way). So, in any case, at this time, in the 1960s, in addition to being all muscled out, Oliver was a serious recreational drug taker. And because he's Oliver, he was extremely curious about his highs, no matter how weird they were. One time, for example, he took twenty pills that he shouldn't have.

SACKS: And then, to my surprise, um, there was a spider on the wall, which said, "Hello!" It had a voice like Bertrand Russell—

A famous mathematician.

SACKS: —and it asked me a while the technical question as to whether Russell had exploded Frager's Paradox, and, um, we had this conversation—

KRULWICH: You answered the spider?

SACKS: Oh, sure, I answered the spider.

KRULWICH: You discussed Frager's Paradox with a spider.

SACKS: I did indeed. Because you trust your perceptions.

KRULWICH: Okay.

SACKS: Many years later, when I mentioned this to an entomologist friend at Cornell, the philosophical spider, he said, "Yes," he said. "I know the species."

So, thinking Oliver's way, taking it all in—talking spiders, whatever—the generosity of his curiosity becomes profoundly moving and transformative when he's treating his patients. I want to tell one story here, really quickly, to demonstrate what I mean.

Oliver once had a patient whom he called Mrs. O. C. She was an old woman, she was eighty-eight years old, living in a nursing home. And one night she was awakened, jarred awake by a loud sound. It was a song. And she thought, Well, somebody's left the radio on, *but when she looked, the radio in the room was off, her roommate sound asleep, which was odd because the song was* really *loud. And after that, there was another song, and then another song, and Mrs. O. C. thought,* Well, maybe my roommate can't hear the song because the songs are coming through the fillings in my teeth, I've heard that's possible. *But, no, her doctors told her, "This is something in your head, you need to see a neurologist," which led her to Dr. Sacks. Now, when he met Mrs. O. C., she could barely hear him. The songs sung by the female voice were coming and coming. She was frightened and justifiably worried that she was going crazy. But Oliver said, "No, no, no, I'm going to do some tests." And when he was done, he said he'd found a slight stroke or condition that had triggered musical epilepsy, the sudden production of music in her brain. Now a normal doctor might say, "Okay, we've got the diagnosis," and think that the songs would probably fade and it would pass, so they would be done. But Oliver did not stop. He doesn't stop. He kept talking to her. She told him she was born in Ireland in the 1890s, her father died before she was born, her mother when she was only five.*

SACKS: Orphaned, alone, she was sent to America to live with a rather forbidding maiden aunt. She had no conscious memory of the first five years of her life. No memory of her mother, of Ireland, and she had always felt this as a keen and painful sadness, this lack, or forgetting of the earliest, most precious years of her life.

So he asked her about the songs, "What are they like?" And Mrs. O. C. said, "Well, I think they're lullabies." "Can you sing them for me?" She did, and then after checking with, I'm not sure who, Oliver figured out that these songs happened to be popular Irish ballads from the 1890s, when Mrs. O. C. was a little baby, and that gave him an idea. And what he does next isn't science, it isn't in any traditional way medicine. He just told her a story. And it goes like this . . .

You know how nobody remembers anything that happens to you when you're one or two or three? Well, there was a theory once, not honored much today, but it said that those earliest memories get locked away deep in our brains in a special safe that we can never open. So let's suppose, Mrs. O. C., that your stroke, by some crazy chance, opened the lock that none of us can break, and released those first memories in you, just for a little while. So that the voice you're listening to . . . maybe that isn't a radio voice. Let's say that it's your mother's voice, that's your missing mother. And so at the ripe old age of eighty-eight, you finally get to be back in your mother's arms, you get to be a baby again. And Mrs. O. C. thought about that and said, "Okay . . . it sort of fits!"

SACKS: I'm an old woman with a stroke, in an old people's home. But I feel I'm a child in Ireland again, I feel my mother's arms, I see her. I hear her voice singing.

Shortly thereafter, the songs began to fade, the pauses widened. Mrs. O. C., who had been so frightened by this music in her head, was now sorry to see the songs go. But it was Oliver who noticed how those songs had touched her, who noticed that the songs might become a comfort to her, because that's what he does: he listens closely. He can hear another person's heart. And this is really the profound puzzle for me of Oliver, because reading the new autobiography, you see that, while he was so full of heart as a doctor, in his own life and in the relationships that really mattered, it turns out he didn't get a whole lot of affection. He was, for a long time, a lonely guy. I would say he was very lonely. And he's talking about that now, for the first time.

KRULWICH: Let me talk about love for a minute. Um, in this book, you tell the story of your very first love, a fellow by the name of Richard Selig. Can you just tell me a little about what happened with him?

SACKS: Um, yeah, he was a Rhodes Scholar at Oxford, and a poet, and handsome—beautiful, beyond belief—and I, sort of, fell for him. Although I didn't say anything because I was, um, very haunted by my mother's accusations.

KRULWICH: What did your mother . . .

SACKS: Um, well, to go a couple of years back, then, my father had opened a conversation. I was about to go to Oxford and it was a sort of a father-son conversation. He said, "You don't seem to have many girlfriends." And I said, "No," wishing the conversation would stop. He said, um, "Something wrong with girls?" And I said, "No, they're fine." "Perhaps you prefer boys?" And I said, "Well, yes, I do." I said, "I've never done anything. But I do." And—

KRULWICH: And you knew that then.

SACKS: I knew that then. I'd known it for six years, probably since I was twelve. Um, and I said, "Don't tell Ma, she won't be able to take it." But my father *did* tell my mother in the night, and the next morning she came down with, um, I somehow want to say *a face of thunder*, and raged at me. And my mother then said, "You're an abomination. I wish you had never been born." And then she suddenly shut up and said nothing for three days. And, um, the matter was never mentioned again in her lifetime. And then, two years later, I found myself for the first time in my life falling in love.

And this was the young guy, Richard. Oliver at the time was in college.

SACKS: It was a very positive feeling, though I didn't know whether it was one which I dared express. But I did say so with my heart and my mouth to Richard.

KRULWICH: What did—do you remember what you said?

SACKS: I, I . . . I said, "I'm in love with you." And, oh, Richard gripped me by the shoulders and he said, "I know." He said, "But I'm not that way. But I love you in my own way." And, um, I was glad I had said it, and glad it had been received in such a warm, friendly way. I thought we might be friends for the rest of our lives. But then one day he came in to me, he said he'd been bothered by finding a lump in his groin . . .

And he was worried.

SACKS: . . . could I have a look at it? And I looked at it, and I felt it, and it was hard and tethered. It turned out to be a particularly malignant form of lymphoid tumor, what's called a lymphosarcoma, and um, he never spoke to me again after that. I don't know whether, since I had been the first to recognize the ominous import, I don't know whether he saw me as a harbinger of death, or a messenger of death, whatever.

KRULWICH: But you were left with that silence?

SACKS: Yeah.

KRULWICH: Yeah.

A few years later, Oliver met a man named Mel. He was young; he was a sailor; like Oliver, he was into weightlifting; they became close friends. And they began living together.

SACKS: I adored him, and was in love with him, and loved physical contact with him.

And they'd work out, and they'd wrestle, and ride motorcycles kind of tightly, and they never talked about what might or might not be happening between them. But one day, they were together, and Oliver was giving Mel a back massage, which Mel often asked him to do.

SACKS: And, um, I loved doing that.

And Oliver said, sometimes he'd get a little, you know, excited . . .

SACKS: And so long as I gave no explicit indication, it was okay. But, but one day, things went a bit too far. And I got sort of, um, I went over the brink, instead of just before the brink. Um, Mel immediately sort of got up, and had a shower, and said, "I can't stay with you anymore." And, um, I found that very cruel, and upsetting, and heartbreaking, and it made me feel, *I don't want to have anything to do with people. I mustn't fall in love. And I cannot share lives with anyone again.*

And he didn't share his life with anyone for a long, long time. In fact, he told me a story about something that happened to him, maybe . . . eight years ago?

SACKS: I was just joining the faculty at Columbia, and I was having a sort of a . . . an interview. And at one point, the interviewer said to me, she said, "I have something rather private to ask you. Would you like Ms. Edgar, your assistant, to leave?" And I said, "No, she's privy to all my affairs." And I then said, thinking she was going to ask me about sex, I said, "I haven't had any sex for thirty-five years." I mean, in fact, she was going to ask me my social security number! And she burst into laughter, and she said, "Oh, you poor thing! We must do something about it."

Well, the truth is, Oliver didn't do anything about it because he didn't think he could. I mean, he had chosen Richard, lost Richard. Chosen Mel, lost Mel. What was the point, he was thinking. And then, finally, and who knows when or why these things happen to people, but a man came along who, for the first time, chose Oliver.

SACKS: I had met Billy as I meet a number of people, because I'd been sent a manuscript or a proof for a book. And, um, an intimacy grew between us. I don't think I quite realized how deep it was, but then there was a particular episode in Christmas of '09, when he came up. And in a sort of serious way he has, a serious, careful way, he said, "I have conceived a deep love for you."

KRULWICH: "I have conceived a deep love for you."

SACKS: Yeah.

KRULWICH: That has a sort of, um . . . that's like got a few extra words. I have *conceived* a deep love for you . . .

SACKS: Right, okay.

KRULWICH: Was he scared to say, "I love you," or—

SACKS: Um, no. He likes the English language. And, um, I think it couldn't have been put more cautiously and yet more strongly. I think it was a beautiful way of putting it. And then I realized, at that moment, with *his* saying that, that I had conceived a deep love for him. And I, um, among other things, I thought, *Good God, it's happened again.* And, *I'm in my seventy-seventh year*—

KRULWICH: That's amazing, seventy-seven.

SACKS: —and, *What next?* And things, basically, have gone happily ever since. And surprisingly guiltlessly. Um, because, then again, I'm not dealing with a *what*, I'm dealing with a *who*. I'm dealing with an individual. I'm not dealing with a, um, with a condition defined by medicine or law.

So Oliver still doesn't know how much time he has left, but for the moment, as you can hear, his mind is totally intact. He's still writing, he has two books in addition to the one you'll find in the lobby, that he's writing, and the children's book, a bunch of New Yorker *stories in the last few months, and a* New York

Review of Books *story. He's got energy to spare. So I want to do one last thing before we close, and this comes from yet another conversation I had with him. And it's a story I know Oliver would hate, because he's not a capital* R *religious kind of guy. But he is somebody who definitely embraces mystery. And for a long time, he's been mystified by a color called* indigo.

SACKS: Indigo, which Newton had inserted between blue and violet. And no two people seem to agree as to what indigo was like. And, um, so I built up a sort of chemical launch pad.

Meaning he took a lot *of drugs.*

SACKS: A base of amphetamines for general arousal, then some acid, and a little cannabis, and when I was sufficiently stoned, I said, "I want to see indigo *now!*" As if in reply, and as if thrown by a giant paintbrush, there appeared a huge, trembling, pear-shaped blob of what I instantly realized was pure indigo, on the white wall in front of me. It had a wonderful luminosity, and in particular, I, although I'm not a religious person, I thought, *This is the color of heaven.* And I limped towards it in a sort of ecstasy, and then suddenly it disappeared.

And he says he had one more moment like that. This time, no drugs. He was at a museum staring at an Egyptian artifact. He sees this radiant color back again, just for a beat.

SACKS: I was given five tantalizing seconds of radiant, ineffable beauty.

And then, again, it vanished.

SACKS: And that was in 1965, and I've never seen indigo since.

But, who knows, you know? Someday, I like to think, Dr. Sacks might get to see that color again.

OLIVER SACKS was born in 1933 in London and was educated at Queen's College, Oxford. He completed his medical training at San Francisco's Mount Zion Hospital and at UCLA before moving to New York, where he soon encountered the patients whom he would write about in his book *Awakenings*. Sacks spent almost fifty years working as a neurologist and wrote many books, including *The Man Who Mistook His Wife for a Hat*, *Musicophilia*, and *Hallucinations*, about the strange neurological predicaments and conditions of his patients. Over the years, he received many awards, including honors from the Guggenheim Foundation, the National Science Foundation, the American Academy of Arts and Letters, and the Royal College of Physicians. He died in 2015.

TERRY GROSS is the host and co–executive producer of *Fresh Air*, an interview-format radio show produced by WHYY-FM in Philadelphia and distributed throughout the United States by NPR.

CHARLIE ROSE is an American television talk show host and journalist. Since 1991, he has hosted *Charlie Rose*, an interview show distributed nationally by PBS.

STUDS TERKEL was an American author, historian, actor, and broadcaster. His well-known radio program, *The Studs Terkel Program*, aired on WFMT Chicago between 1952 and 1997. He won a Pulitzer Prize for General Non-Fiction in 1985. He died in 2008.

LISA BURRELL is a senior editor at *Harvard Busines Review*.

TOM ASHBROOK is an American journalist and radio broadcaster. He hosts the nationally syndicated, public radio call-in program *On Point*.

ROBERT KRULWICH is an award-winning journalist and cohost of *Radiolab*.

THE LAST INTERVIEW SERIES

KURT VONNEGUT: THE LAST INTERVIEW

"I think it can be tremendously refreshing if a creator of literature has something on his mind other than the history of literature so far. Literature should not disappear up its own asshole, so to speak."

$15.95 / $17.95 CAN
978-1-61219-090-7
ebook: 978-1-61219-091-4

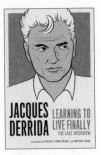

LEARNING TO LIVE FINALLY: THE LAST INTERVIEW
JACQUES DERRIDA

"I am at war with myself, it's true, you couldn't possibly know to what extent . . . I say contradictory things that are, we might say, in real tension; they are what construct me, make me live, and will make me die."

translated by PASCAL-ANNE BRAULT and MICHAEL NAAS

$15.95 / $17.95 CAN
978-1-61219-094-5
ebook: 978-1-61219-032-7

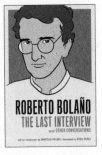

ROBERTO BOLAÑO: THE LAST INTERVIEW

"Posthumous: It sounds like the name of a Roman gladiator, an unconquered gladiator. At least that's what poor Posthumous would like to believe. It gives him courage."

translated by SYBIL PEREZ and others

$15.95 / $17.95 CAN
978-1-61219-095-2
ebook: 978-1-61219-033-4

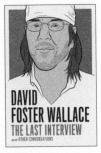

DAVID FOSTER WALLACE: THE LAST INTERVIEW

"I don't know what you're thinking or what it's like inside you and you don't know what it's like inside me. In fiction . . . we can leap over that wall itself in a certain way."

$15.95 / $15.95 CAN
978-1-61219-206-2
ebook: 978-1-61219-207-9

THE LAST INTERVIEW SERIES

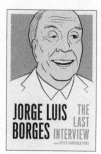

JORGE LUIS BORGES: THE LAST INTERVIEW

"Believe me: the benefits of blindness have been greatly
exaggerated. If I could see, I would never leave the
house, I'd stay indoors reading the many books that
surround me."

translated by KIT MAUDE

$15.95 / $15.95 CAN
978-1-61219-204-8
ebook: 978-1-61219-205-5

HANNAH ARENDT: THE LAST INTERVIEW

"There are no dangerous thoughts for the simple reason
that thinking itself is such a dangerous enterprise."

$15.95 / $15.95 CAN
978-1-61219-311-3
ebook: 978-1-61219-312-0

RAY BRADBURY: THE LAST INTERVIEW

"You don't have to destroy books to destroy a culture.
Just get people to stop reading them."

$15.95 / $15.95 CAN
978-1-61219-421-9
ebook: 978-1-61219-422-6

JAMES BALDWIN: THE LAST INTERVIEW

"You don't realize that you're intelligent
until it gets you into trouble."

$15.95 / $15.95 CAN
978-1-61219-400-4
ebook: 978-1-61219-401-1

THE LAST INTERVIEW SERIES

GABRIEL GÁRCIA MÁRQUEZ: THE LAST INTERVIEW

"The only thing the Nobel Prize is good for is not having to wait in line."

$15.95 / $15.95 CAN
978-1-61219-480-6
ebook: 978-1-61219-481-3

LOU REED: THE LAST INTERVIEW

"Hubert Selby. William Burroughs. Allen Ginsberg. Delmore Schwartz . . . I thought if you could do what those writers did and put it to drums and guitar, you'd have the greatest thing on earth."

$15.95 / $15.95 CAN
978-1-61219-478-3
ebook: 978-1-61219-479-0

ERNEST HEMINGWAY: THE LAST INTERVIEW

"The most essential gift for a good writer is a built-in, shockproof, shit detector."

$15.95 / $20.95 CAN
978-1-61219-522-3
ebook: 978-1-61219-523-0

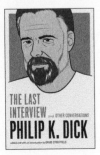

PHILIP K. DICK: THE LAST INTERVIEW

"The basic thing is, how frightened are you of chaos? And how happy are you with order?"

$15.95 / $20.95 CAN
978-1-61219-526-1
ebook: 978-1-61219-527-8

THE LAST INTERVIEW SERIES

NORA EPHRON: THE LAST INTERVIEW

"You better *make* them care about what you think.
It had better be quirky or perverse or thoughtful
enough so that you hit some chord in them. Otherwise,
it doesn't work."

$15.95 / $20.95 CAN
978-1-61219-524-7
ebook: 978-1-61219-525-4

JANE JACOBS: THE LAST INTERVIEW

"I would like it to be understood that all our human
economic achievements have been done by ordinary
people, not by exceptionally educated people, or by
elites, or by supernatural forces."

$15.95 / $20.95 CAN
978-1-61219-534-6
ebook: 978-1-61219-535-3